ISS  I0059436

Dediu Newsletter

Author: Michael M. Dediu

Monthly news, reviews, comments and suggestions for a better and wiser world

Volume 1, Number 1, 6 December 2016

DERC Publishing House

Tewksbury (Boston), Massachusetts, U. S. A.

For subscriptions please use the contact form at www.derc.com

Published and printed in the
United States of America
On the Great Seal of the United States are included:
E Pluribus Unum (Out of many, one)
Annuit Coeptis (He has approved of the undertakings)
Novus Ordo Seclorum (New order of the ages)

Dediu, Michael M.

Dediu Newsletter Vol 1, Number 1, 6 Dec 2016
Monthly reviews, comments and suggestions for a better and
wiser world

ISSN 2475-2061
ISBN 978-1-939757-40-1

Preface

We start this newsletter in order to bring to the general public monthly significant news from many countries, reviews, comments and suggestions, for a better and wiser world. We included also some nice photos.

I want to thank my wife Sophia for her assistance.

There are many important news in different countries, and any reader, no matter from what part of the world, will surely find, in this newsletter of general interest, numerous relevant and useful facts and images.

Michael M. Dediu, Ph. D.

Boston, U. S. A., 6 December 2016

Table of Contents

United States of America

The White House blocked a Chinese company from buying the German company Aixtron (a chip equipment maker), for the reason that the U.S. defense contractor Northrop Grumman, is a customer of Aixtron. In over 25 years, only twice the White House vetoed an investment by an overseas buyer in an overseas company, because of a national security threat.

President-Elect Trump insists that he will drain the swamp and will change policies.

President-elect Donald Trump accepted a congratulatory phone call from Taiwan's President Tsai Ing-wen, which is regarded by China as a breaking of nearly four decades of U.S foreign policy of "One China." On 3 December, President-elect Trump also spoke out against China on Twitter, accusing Beijing of manipulating its currency, unfairly taxing U.S. products, and militarizing the South China Sea.

Specialists in education say that President-Elect Trump has the option to increase the educational choice, in other words, a choice plan should concentrate on optimizing instructional choices, not just school choices.

California, Massachusetts, Vermont, Hawaii, Maryland, New York, Illinois, Rhode Island, New Jersey, and Connecticut lost people due to domestic migration (excluding immigration), over the last 10 years (2004-2014). Nearly 2.75 millions more Americans left California and New York than entered these states.

Washington, D.C. (1790): George Washington (1732-1799, first President 1789-1797) Monument (1848-1885, 169 m, 43 ha), on the National Mall, 700 m south of the White House, seen from the Constitution Avenue NW.

China, Japan, and neighbors

China: After the election, President of the People's Republic of China, Xi Jinping, called President-elect Trump to congratulate him.

Chinese President Xi Jinping has called for a smaller army with better combat capability and optimized structure, as the military reform deepens.

Chinese President Xi Jinping is also General Secretary, Communist Party of China Central Committee, Chairman, Communist Party of China Central Military Commission, and Chairman, People's Republic of China Central Military Commission.

China will help Sierra Leone improve its industrialization and public health system, President Xi Jinping said on 1 December.

On 28 November Chinese President Xi Jinping called on China and Latin American countries to strengthen dialogue on global issues, and boost cooperation on domestic development, in a bid to better build their community of common destiny on a new starting point in history.

Chinese President Xi Jinping's keynote speech at the Asia Pacific Economic Cooperation (APEC) CEO Summit on Saturday 26 November, in Lima, Peru, placed China and the region at the forefront of a joint effort to reactivate the global economy, APEC participants and scholars have said.

Shenzhen is Asia's busiest stock exchange, with monthly turnover of more than $1 T, and The Shenzhen-Hong Kong Stock Connect started on 5 December. Shanghai stock exchange is two years old and has big volumes of trades.

Interpol names Chinese Police Official as its new President.

Missile defense experts at the US company Raytheon Co. will upgrade a long-range surveillance radar system in Taiwan, which has been in operation since early 2013, to help warn the island of attacks.

Japan: After the election, Prime Minister of Japan, Shinzō Abe, called President-elect Trump to congratulate him.

South Korea: after many protests against corruption, the President will step down in April 2017. Military avionics experts at the U.S. company Lockheed Martin Corp. will upgrade South Korea's 134 KF-16 jet fighters under terms of a $1.2 billion U.S. Air Force contract.

Tokyo, Shinjuku. Center-left: Tokyo Opera City Tower (234 m, 54 floors, 1996); right Shinjuku Mitsui Building (224 m, 55 floors, 1974),

Russia, Switzerland, Eastern Europe

Russia: On 14 November, President-elect Donald J. Trump spoke with President of Russia Vladimir Putin, who called to offer his congratulations on winning the election. During the call, the two leaders discussed a range of issues, including the threats and challenges facing the United States and Russia, strategic economic issues, and the historical U.S.-Russia relationship that dates back over 200 years. President-elect Trump noted to President Putin that he is very much looking forward to having a strong and enduring relationship with Russia and the people of Russia.

On 2 December, Russian President Vladimir Putin opened the Fifth St Petersburg International Cultural Forum.

On 2 December, Russian President Vladimir Putin had a meeting with the Foreign Minister of Japan, Fumio Kishida.

On Wednesday 30 November, Russian President Vladimir Putin had a telephone conversation with President of Turkey, Recep Tayyip Erdogan.

On Tuesday 29 November, Russian President Vladimir Putin instructed the Defense Ministry and the Ministry of Civil Defense, Emergencies and Disaster Relief to set up field hospitals in Syria, with the purpose of providing medical assistance to the residents of Aleppo and nearby territories. This task is to be implemented within the shortest possible timeframe, as per the decision of the President. Specifically, the Defense Ministry will send a special medical detachment along with a multi-purpose field hospital with 100 places, and a special pediatric unit. The hospital will have a capacity to provide outpatient medical services to 420 people a day. The Emergencies Ministry will transport a field hospital with 50 places, which will provide inpatient medical services, and will have a capacity to provide outpatient medical services to 200 people a day.

Russian army will receive an advanced stealth drone hunter.

Poland: After the election, President of Poland, Andrzej Duda, called President-elect Trump to congratulate him.

Greece has a debt of €86 B.

Switzerland: The President of the Confederation (German: Bundespräsident der Eidgenossenschaft, French: Président de la Confédération, Italian: Presidente della Confederazione, Romansh: President da la Confederaziun) is the presiding member of the seven-member Swiss Federal Council. The office does not confer the status of head of state, which is held jointly by all the councillors. Johann Schneider-Amman, the president for 2016, has been trade minister and a Federal Council member since 2010, representing the liberal Free Democratic Party. Term length: 1 year, not eligible for re-election.

Geneva (121 BC under Romans), Avenue de la Paix 19, International Committee of the Red Cross, founded by Jean Henri Dunant (1828-1910) on Feb. 9, 1863, three Nobel Peace Prizes.

United Kingdom, Canada, South America

United Kingdom: It seems that UK may trigger the Article 50 process to leave the EU by the end of March 2917, even if the result of a UK Supreme Court appeal will be negative. Former members of the Remain campaign will continue to resist.

Canada: After the election, Prime Minister of Canada, Justin Trudeau, called President-elect Trump to congratulate him.

Mexico: After the election, President of Mexico, Enrique Peña Nieto, called President-elect Trump to congratulate him.

Peru: On 28 November, visiting Chinese President Xi Jinping and his Peruvian counterpart, Pedro Pablo Kuczynski, pledged to boost bilateral cultural exchanges and mutual learning between China-Latin America and Caribbean civilizations.

London, England: the statue The St Saviour's War Memorial, and the Shard (2009-2013, 309.6 m, observatory at 244.3 m, 95 floors (72 habitable), 110K m², 44 elevators)

France, Germany, and neighbors

France: The President of France Francois Hollande said that he will not seek re-election for a second term in the Presidential election from 2017 in France. From the Elysée Palace he said that there is a risk of not being able to unite people behind his candidacy. The current candidates are Francois Fillon and Marine Le Pen.

The Netherlands: After the election, Prime Minister of The Netherlands, Mark Rutte, called President-elect Trump to congratulate him.

Sweden: After the election, Prime Minister of Sweden, Stefan Löfven, called President-elect Trump to congratulate him.

Germany: from 2012, the President of the Federal Republic of Germany is Joachim Gauck.

Place de la Concorde (1772): The Egyptian obelisk (Ramses the Great, 1250 BC, 23 m), Marine Nationale (Navy, 1758, left).

India, Pakistan, Australia, and neighbors

India: After the election, Prime Minister of the Republic of India, Narendra Modi, called President-elect Trump to congratulate him.

Australia: After the election, Prime Minister of the Commonwealth of Australia, Malcolm Turnbull, called President-elect Trump to congratulate him.

New Zealand: on 5 December New Zealand Prime Minister John Key announced he would not seek a fourth term. Key has been in power since 2008, and is backing his finance minister, Bill English, to take the controls.

Pakistan: on 30 November the President-elect Trump and the Prime Minister of Pakistan Muhammad Nawaz Sharif spoke on the phone. They had a productive conversation about how the United States and Pakistan will have a strong working relationship in the future.

Thailand: after the recent passing of his father Bhumibol, who reigned for seven decades, Crown Prince Maha Vajiralongkorn has been proclaimed the new King of Thailand. The Bank of Thailand left its growth forecast for 2016 unchanged at 3.2%.

Australia, Sydney (1788, 5 M people), from the Royal Botanic Gardens looking northwest to the southeast side of the harbourfront Sydney Opera House (1959-1973, 183 m by 120 m by 65 m height, total seating capacity 5738)) and the Sydney Harbour Bridge (1932, left).

Italy, Middle East, Africa

Italy: After the election, Prime Minister of Italy, Matteo Renzi, called President-elect Trump to congratulate him.

Because he lost the referendum on Sunday, the 4th of December (over 59% of Italians voted to block his constitutional reform plans (to reduce the power of the Senate)), Prime Minister of Italy, Matteo Renzi, saying that the people have spoken in a clear and unequivocal way, and he leaves with no regrets, went to Palazzo Quirinale, to the President of Italy, Sergio Mattarella, to tender his resignation. However the Italian President Sergio Mattarella asked him to delay his resignation until the Senate passes his government's 2017 budget. President Mattarella also indicated that he won't call sudden elections in response to the referendum results, stating it was important for Italy's institutions to respect commitments and deadlines, and it would take time to find the right solutions.

The Bank of Italy estimates there is €360 B worth of non-performing loans in the Italian banking system.

Among the biggest winners of the referendum is the anti-establishment 5 Star Movement, which has called for a nonbinding plebiscite on Italy's euro membership. Italy has already seen 63 governments in just 70 years.

Jordan: After the election, King Abdullah II bin Al Hussein of Jordan, called President-elect Trump to congratulate him.

Iran said that the U.S. Senate's vote, to extend the Iran Sanctions Act for another decade, is a violation of the 2015 agreement with six major powers, which restricted its nuclear program.

Egypt: After the election, President of the Arab Republic of Egypt, Abdel Fattah al-Sisi, called President-elect Trump to congratulate him.

Italy, Rome, Trajan's column was erected in 113 AD in honor of Emperor Trajan. It is located at the Forum of Trajan. The column commemorates Trajan's victories in Dacia (now Romania), and is 42 meters tall, including its base.

Too fat?

As we all know, obesity is a big issue for many people. Well, eating less is an idea, or, maybe eating dinner early, or just skipping it all together, may actually help a little in fighting body fat.

USA, University of California, Berkeley (1868), School of Public Policy (1893, 2002), at 2607 Hearst Avenue, north of Evans Hall.

Too much salt?

I noticed in many occasions that people, and especially children, consume too much salt. It is well known that this is risky, because it may contribute to high blood pressure and increased cardiovascular problems. I, for one, follow doctor's advice, and eat less salt.

Hypertension, which is chronically elevated blood pressure, effects about 70 million Americans, putting them at an increased risk for developing heart disease or having a stroke. Almost everyone believes that lowering salt in the diet can lower a person's blood pressure, but despite that belief and decades of warnings from government agencies, health organizations, and our doctors, Americans still eat about 1,000 mg of sodium a day more than the recommended limit of 2,300 mg.

Japan, Osaka (645), from Shin-Osaka Washington Hotel Plaza, looking south to Yodo River and buildings north (down) and south.

Mathematics and MRI

In Mathematical Reviews there many interesting reviews of important articles. It is fascinating to see what a big role the mathematics has in the signal and image processing domains (where natural images can be represented efficiently as piecewise smooth functions), magnetic resonance images (MRI), and in computer vision, especially regarding the problem of image recovery.

USA, University of California, Berkeley (1868), Mathematical Sciences Research Institute (1982), at 17 Gauss Way, on the hill.

Satellites

Now there are 1,419 operational satellites, which are currently in orbit. The US company SpaceX intends to deploy 4,425 satellites, in order to create a super-fast global internet network. That's more than three times the current number of satellites.

Satellites that are further away travel slower. The International Space Station has a Low Earth Orbit, about 400 kilometers above the Earth's surface. Objects orbiting at that altitude travel about 28,000 km/h.

People at equator rotate with a speed of 465 m/s.

A satellite near equator has a speed of 7.9 km/s.

Geostationary satellites: 3.1 km/s.

The Moon rotates in its orbit with a speed of 1km/s.

USA, Washington, D.C. (1790): the Lunar Module Eagle from Apollo 11 (1969), at the National Air and Space Museum (1976).

Food and robots

The food industry will intensify the use of robots.

Generally speaking, robots can be autonomous or semi-autonomous, and range from humanoids (Honda's Advanced Step in Innovative Mobility (ASIMO) and TOSY's TOSY Ping Pong Playing Robot (TOPIO)), to industrial robots, medical operating robots, patent assist robots, therapy robots, collectively programmed *swarm* robots, UAV drones, microscopic nano robots and many others.

USA, Washington, D.C. (1790): the 1903 Wright Flyer airplane, at The National Air and Space Museum (1976) of the Smithsonian Institution, between Jefferson Dr SW and Independence Ave SW.

Michael M. Dediu is also the author of these books (which can be found on Amazon.com):

1. Aphorisms and quotations – with examples and explanations
2. Axioms, aphorisms and quotations – with examples and explanations
3. 100 Great Personalities and their Quotations
4. Professor Petre P. Teodorescu – A Great Mathematician and Engineer
5. Professor Ioan Goia – A Dedicated Engineering Professor
6. Venice (Venezia) – a new perspective. A short presentation with photographs
7. La Serenissima (Venice) - a new photographic perspective. A short presentation with many photos
8. Grand Canal – Venice. A new photographic viewpoint. A short presentation with many photos
9. Piazza San Marco – Venice. A different photographic view. A short presentation with many photos
10. Roma (Rome) - La Città Eterna. A new photographic view. A short presentation with many photos
11. Why is Rome so Fascinating? A short presentation with many photos
12. Rome, Boston and Helsinki. A short photographic presentation
13. Rome and Tokyo – two captivating cities. A short photographic presentation
14. Beautiful Places on Earth – A new photographic presentation
15. From Niagara Falls to Mount Fuji via Rome - A novel photographic presentation
16. From the USA and Canada to Italy and Japan - A fresh photographic presentation
17. Paris – Why So Many Call This City Mon Amour - A lovely photographic presentation
18. The City of Light – Paris (La Ville-Lumière) - A kaleidoscopic photographic presentation
19. Paris (Lutetia Parisiorum) – the romance capital of the world - A kaleidoscopic photographic view
20. Paris and Tokyo – a joyful photographic presentation. With a preamble about the Universe

21. From USA to Japan via Canada – A cheerful photographic documentary

22. 200 Wonderful Places, In The Last 50 Years – A personal photographic documentary

23. Must see places in USA and Japan - A kaleidoscopic photographic documentary

24. Grandeurs of the World - A kaleidoscopic photographic documentary

25. Corneliu Leu – writer on the same wavelength as Mark Twain. An American viewpoint

26. From Berkeley to Pompeii via Rome – A kaleidoscopic photographic documentary

27. From America to Europe via Japan - A kaleidoscopic photographic documentary

28. Discover America and Japan - A photographic documentary

29. J. R. Lucas – philosopher on a creative parallel with Plato, An American viewpoint

30. From America to Switzerland via France - A photographic documentary

31. From Bretton Woods to New York via Cape Cod - A photographic documentary

32. Splendid Places on the Atlantic Coast of the U. S. A. - A photographic documentary

33. Fourteen nice Cities on three Continents - A photographic documentary

34. 17 Picturesque Cities on the World Map - A photographic documentary

35. Unforgettable Places from Four Continents including Trump buildings - A photographic documentary

Michael M. Dediu is the editor of these books (also on Amazon.com):

1. Sophia Dediu: The life and its torrents – Ana. In Europe around 1920
2. Proceedings of the 4th International Conference "Advanced Composite Materials Engineering" COMAT 2012
3. Adolf Shvedchikov: I am an eternal child of spring – poems in English, Italian, French, German, Spanish and Russian
4. Adolf Shvedchikov: Life's Enigma – poems in English, Italian and Russian
5. Adolf Shvedchikov: Everyone wants to be HAPPY – poems in English, Spanish and Russian
6. Adolf Shvedchikov: My Life, My Love – poems in English, Italian and Russian
7. Adolf Shvedchikov: I am the gardener of love – poems in English and Russian
8. Adolf Shvedchikov: Amaretta di Saronno – poems in English and Russian
9. Adolf Shvedchikov: A Russian Rediscovers America
10. Adolf Shvedchikov: Parade of Life - poems in English and Russian
11. Adolf Shvedchikov: Overcoming Sorrow - poems in English and Russian
12. Sophia Dediu: Sophia meets Japan
13. Corneliu Leu: Roosevelt, Churchill, Stalin and Hitler: Their surprising role in Eastern Europe in 1944
14. Proceedings of the 5th International Conference "Computational Mechanics and Virtual Engineering" COMEC 2013
15. Georgeta Simion – Potanga: Beyond Imagination: A Thought-provoking novel inspired from mid-20th century events
16. Ana Dediu: The poetry of my life in Europe and The USA
17. Ana Dediu: The Four Graces
18. Proceedings of the 5th International Conference "Advanced Composite Materials Engineering" COMAT 2014
19. Sophia Dediu: Chocolate Cook Book: Is there such a thing as too much chocolate?

20. Sorin Vlase: Mechanical Identifiability in Automotive Engineering

21. Gabriel Dima: The Evolution of the Aerostructures – Concept and Technologies

22. Proceedings of the 6th International Conference "Computational Mechanics and Virtual Engineering" COMEC 2015

23. Sophia Dediu: Cook Book 1 A-B-C Common sense cooking

Washington, D.C. (1790): Douglas DC-3 (1936) airplanes, at The National Air and Space Museum (1976) of the Smithsonian Institution, between Jefferson Dr SW and Independence Ave SW.

www.ingramcontent.com/pod-product-compliance
Lightning Source LLC
Chambersburg PA
CBHW041719200326
41520CB00001B/162